The Mayflower Story

by Tom Streissguth

Content Consultant

Maura Jane Farrelly

Associate Professor and Chair of American Studies
Brandeis University

Famous
Ships

Essential Library

An Imprint of Abdo Publishing | abdopublishing.com

abdopublishing.com

Published by Abdo Publishing, a division of ABDO, PO Box 398166, Minneapolis, Minnesota 55439. Copyright © 2018 by Abdo Consulting Group, Inc. International copyrights reserved in all countries. No part of this book may be reproduced in any form without written permission from the publisher. Essential Library™ is a trademark and logo of Abdo Publishing.

Printed in the United States of America, North Mankato, Minnesota
102017
012018

Cover Photo: Bettmann/Getty Images
Interior Photos: Joseph Sohm/Science Source, 4–5; North Wind Picture Archives, 9, 26, 28–29, 35, 38–39, 43, 50–51, 68–69, 84; Oleg Albinsky/iStockphoto, 11; Bumi Hills/Shutterstock Images, 12–13; Andreas Juergensmeier/Shutterstock Images, 17, 20; Science & Society Picture Library/SSPL/Getty Images, 20–21; Stillman Rogers/Alamy, 21; Mark Dunn/Alamy, 25; Peter Horree/Alamy, 33; John Nordell/The Christian Science Monitor/Getty Images, 40; Trinity Mirror/Mirrorpix/Alamy, 44; Ann Ronan Pictures/Print Collector/Hulton Archive/Getty Images, 47; Royal Astronomical Society/Science Source, 53; Michael Ventura/Alamy, 55; Michael Doolittle/Alamy, 57; iStockphoto, 60–61; Michael Gordon/Shutterstock Images, 64; Shutterstock Images, 72; Rischgitz/Hulton Fine Art Collection/Getty Images, 76–77; Herbert Orth/The LIFE Images Collection/Getty Images, 79; David L Ryan/The Boston Globe/Getty Images, 86–87; Red Line Editorial, 91; A. F. Archive/Alamy, 95; Denis Tangney Jr./iStockphoto, 97

Editor: Rebecca Rowell
Series Designer: Craig Hinton

Publisher's Cataloging-in-Publication Data

Names: Streissguth, Tom, author.
Title: The Mayflower story / by Tom Streissguth.
Description: Minneapolis, Minnesota : Abdo Publishing, 2018. | Series: Famous ships | Includes online resources and index.
Identifiers: LCCN 2017946751 | ISBN 9781532113208 (lib.bdg.) | ISBN 9781532152085 (ebook)
Subjects: LCSH: Mayflower (Ship)--Juvenile literature. | Massachusetts--History--New Plymouth, 1620-1691--Juvenile literature. | Pilgrims (New Plymouth Colony)--Juvenile literature.
Classification: DDC 974.48202--dc23
LC record available at https://lccn.loc.gov/2017946751

Contents

⚓ *The* Mayflower II, *a modern replica of the original ship, helps people understand what the Pilgrims might have experienced during their historic journey on the* Mayflower.

ARRIVAL IN THE NEW WORLD

A squat, three-masted sailing ship drew close to a long, low strip of beach. The rough and cold waters of the North Atlantic Ocean were breaking along the shore. On the other side of this peninsula was Cape Cod Bay. It was November 11, 1620—very late in the season for ocean sailing. The ship pitched and rolled in the waves. Its passengers remained below decks, seeking shelter in their cramped and airless quarters.

With Master Christopher Jones in command, the *Mayflower* had just completed a difficult voyage across the North Atlantic. The ship had taken a northern track to avoid pirates—who preferred fairer weather and seas. But Jones and his crew had fought westerly gales that blew against their course. No ports had been available for repairs or provisions during the trek. Passengers and crew had seen nothing but sea, sky, and clouds. Many of the passengers had suffered the awful miseries of seasickness, and others were ill with life-threatening diseases. A crewman had died, as had one of the passengers.

A baby had been born. For an ordinary English merchant ship of the 1600s, the 66-day journey had been a very long voyage.

Exploring the Hudson

The *Mayflower*'s passengers originally intended to settle at the mouth of the Hudson River. They would not be the first Europeans to reach that river. In 1609, English sea captain Henry Hudson had explored what became known as the Hudson Valley. He was working for the Dutch East India Company, a group of merchants. Sailing as far north as the site of Albany (in present-day New York), Hudson claimed the river and the entire valley for the company.

Off Nantucket

Two days earlier, the *Mayflower* had first dropped anchor in these same heavy seas. It had missed its original destination, the northern reaches of the Virginia Colony at the Hudson River, by more than 200 miles (320 km).[1] Instead of risking a wintry passage south to the Hudson, however, Jones had decided to land his passengers where they landed and remain with them until suitable sailing weather returned in the spring.

Some of the 102 passengers were devoutly religious people.[2] They had come for the purpose of worshipping freely. They were Separatists who had left the Church of England, an act that, in their time, was against the law. Others were English colonists who simply wanted to make a fresh start in the New World. The Separatists knew this group as the Strangers. Collectively, the *Mayflower* passengers are commonly known as the Pilgrims.

Jones's decision to halt the *Mayflower*'s journey at Cape Cod after the initial landing in North America was a fateful one. It might have been a relief to the Separatists. Virginia was still under the king's authority, so they would have been subject to royal decrees. The Separatists might still be persecuted for their religious beliefs.

The Pilgrims did not all agree on this destination, however. Landing at this remote spot and forming

Separatists, Saints, and Puritans

Separatists was a term used during the 1600s, though some considered it derogatory. Members of this religious group knew themselves as "Saints."[3] These colonists and the larger group known today as Pilgrims were not Puritans, another group of devoutly religious New World settlers. Unlike the Separatists, Puritans remained members of the Church of England, conforming to English law. Their goal was to improve and "purify" the church by living closer to the tenets of early Christianity. They sought to establish a better form of English Christianity in North America. In 1630, ten years after the Separatists established Plymouth, the Puritans landed at what became Salem and Charlestown and founded the Massachusetts Bay Colony.

Late to the Party

The *Mayflower* was not the first European ship to reach New England. European fishing boats had been sailing the waters off New England for centuries, even before Christopher Columbus arrived in the New World in 1492. The Basques, a people from northwestern Spain and part of France, were renowned for their great hauls of cod.

Some people in Massachusetts believe a rumor that the *Mayflower* may have been a latecomer to their shores, well behind the arrival of people from elsewhere in Europe. The theory was eagerly taken up by the poet Henry Wadsworth Longfellow and other prominent citizens of Boston, Massachusetts, in the 1800s. For this reason, Boston has a monument to Leif Ericsson, a Viking explorer, looking out over Commonwealth Avenue. According to the monument, Ericsson may have built a settlement in the area six centuries before the Pilgrims arrived. Historians do not give the idea much attention because no physical or archival evidence has been found to support it.

⚓ *An artist depicted some of the people from the* Mayflower *heading to shore in the New World. It would have been a thrilling and nerve-wracking experience.*

a settlement on land for which they had no charter were not in their plan. They wished to continue the journey to the region they had legally been approved to settle. With land in sight, they could surely hunt game or catch fish for food, if needed, and find fresh water during their journey south to the mouth of the Hudson River.

The crew of the *Mayflower* saw things differently. They did not look kindly on the chore of ferrying emigrants to the New World. The Pilgrims had baggage and equipment that claimed the space below decks and prevented the crew from storing and trading their own goods. The sailors had a long winter ahead and would need to safeguard the provisions they had. Whether the Pilgrims stayed in New England or Virginia did not matter to the sailors, who did not relish any further

sailing along the coast. Instead, they would remain safely aboard their ship until Jones gave the order to raise sail and return to England.

Even before setting a single foot on land, the Pilgrims were roiled in argument. Most had staked everything they owned on the Plymouth Company. The voyage was a business venture and a religious pilgrimage. And the Pilgrims had agreed to give all profits made for seven years to the company. Failure would probably ruin the Pilgrims financially.

But Jones had made his decision. Before any settlement could take place, the settlers would have to scout the land. They needed to find fresh water and a safe, sheltered harbor. They needed suitable planting ground and fertile soil. They also had to prepare for an encounter with the native inhabitants, wherever they might be.

The day of their arrival was a Saturday. Sunday was a day for rest and prayer. Even after their long sea voyage, the passengers remained aboard the *Mayflower*. On Monday, November 13, Jones, several passengers, and crew members climbed into a lighter, smaller boat used for shore parties. They raised the boat's lone sail, began to row, and headed for shore, uncertain of what they might find.

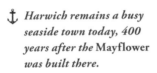
⚓ *Harwich remains a busy seaside town today, 400 years after the Mayflower was built there.*

THE ORIGIN OF THE *MAYFLOWER*

The coastal town of Harwich lies on England's eastern coast. At this spot, the Stour and Orwell Rivers empty into the North Sea. Approximately 30 miles (50 km) to the south is the mouth of the Thames, the river that flows through the vast, bustling port of London, England.

In the early 1500s, Harwich was a fishing port. It grew larger and busier as trade with Asia and the Americas increased. Merchants of the town docked their ships in Harwich's harbor to shelter them from the North Sea's strong winds and turbulent waves. Shipbuilding works fashioned and launched new vessels. In approximately 1600, Harwich became the birthplace of the *Mayflower*.

A New Fluyt

The *Mayflower* was modeled after a popular Dutch ship design known as a *fluyt*. Vessels with this design extended approximately 100 to 130 feet (30 to 40 m) from stem to stern, or front to

The Fluyt

In the 1500s, England and the Netherlands were rivals in the shipbuilding arts. With the fluyt, the Dutch shipwrights, for a time, took the lead. First built in 1595 in the port of Hoorn, the Netherlands, the fluyt was a new kind of large seagoing vessel. It was built strictly for trade, not as a fighting ship.

The merchants of the Dutch East India Company were building new colonies in distant Asia and needed an efficient cargo ship. The fluyt fit the bill perfectly. The typical fluyt carried 35 crew members and officers.[1] With their pear-shaped profile and wide hull, fluyts could carry twice the cargo of older vessels. Because of the relatively small area of sail, they could also save on labor costs and hire fewer sailors to manage them at sea than older ships.

The fluyt also had stepped, or higher, decks fore and aft. This was done for an important reason. Tolls through the straits to the Baltic Sea were based on the size of the main deck. The short main deck of the fluyt saved money for its owners on these expensive tolls.

back.[2] They carried three masts and six sails. They had a tall superstructure, which looked like a small, flat-roofed house, built over the main deck at the back of the ship. The fluyt was a squat, stable, pear-shaped boat with plenty of space for cargo below decks.

At the time of its launch, the *Mayflower* joined England's large and growing merchant fleet. This fleet was England's only means to carry on foreign trade, on which the island kingdom depended for its livelihood. To buy and sell goods, merchants in Harwich, London, Southampton, and other ports sent their vessels to the European continent, as well as Asia, Africa, and the Americas.

During the reign of Queen Elizabeth I (1558–1603), the English had just ended a long, drawn-out war with the kingdom of Spain. England and Spain remained rivals for control of distant colonies and command of the seas. With a far smaller navy, the English had to depend on merchant ships to arm themselves and take part in seaborne campaigns. For this reason, Queen Elizabeth had the legal right to press the *Mayflower* into military service, although no record suggests the ship ever went to war. Because they could be called into military service, the *Mayflower* and other fluyts of the time were built with cannon ports, or windows, along a gun deck, directly below the main deck.

Raising the Mayflower

The building of the *Mayflower* began with the laying of a keel. This long, heavy wooden beam ran the length of the ship at its lowest point in the water. Next, builders attached a stempost to one end of the keel and a sternpost to the other. They added a series of wooden beams to create the frame of the ship's hull. Workers nailed a covering of planks to the frame, coating them with tar to prevent water leaks.

The *Mayflower*, like many other merchant ships, carried three tall masts. A foremast and mainmast were fitted with horizontal yardarms (yards), wooden beams used to support the sails. When unfurled, or untied and open, the sails caught the wind and strained the masts forward, driving the ship through the water. The crew could adjust the yards to catch the wind when it was blowing from port, which is the left side of a ship, or starboard, which is the right side.

The mizzenmast, at the rear of the ship, was lateen rigged. A large triangular sail was unfurled from a long yard set vertically, at an angle to the deck. Having a single sail set on the mizzenmast and fewer sails to work across the ship meant fewer crew members were needed, which saved labor expenses. A bowsprit pointed from the forward bow, or front, of the ship. This spar, or pole, carried a spritsail, which was a square sail set below the bowsprit. A stout line running to the front of the bowsprit anchored the foremast.

Jobs on the Mayflower

No records kept by Master Jones or for the 1620–1621 voyage of the *Mayflower* have survived. But the ship carried the customary crewmen for a 1600s merchant ship. Second in rank to the master were two mates, John Clarke and Robert Coppin, who were also pilots. They gave orders directly to the crew, which included helmsmen who controlled the rudder and steered the boat. The *Mayflower* also carried a surgeon, a carpenter, and a boatswain, who was in charge of the sails and sailing equipment. Four quartermasters kept the stores, and a cooper maintained the casks, hogsheads, and other containers. A swabber kept the decks clean and the ship orderly. Ordinary seamen and younger apprentices handled the sails and rigging.

Under full sail and with a following wind, the *Mayflower* could travel almost 50 miles (80 km) in a day.[3] With a contrary wind, however, the ship would go slower and might make no progress for days. In a heavy storm, the master would order all sails lowered, allowing the ship to drift. Trying to use the sails in a storm was risky. A gusting wind could shred the sails or damage the masts and yards.

Sailors maneuvered the ship's sails by handling the lines, or ropes, that led up to the yards. To unfurl or furl, or tie up, the sails, they climbed a set of ratlines tied to the masts and walked along footropes slung from the bottom of the yards. It was a dangerous business, especially in a strong wind or a storm. Sailors of the *Mayflower*'s time had to be strong, fearless, and sure footed.

Below and Above Decks

The *Mayflower* had two lower decks that ran the length of the ship. The gun deck, directly below the main deck, had gun ports. These small windows allowed gunners to aim and fire their cannon at enemy ships. In the *Mayflower*'s time, a merchant ship—even one that sailed close to home—had to be able to defend itself, even when not in military service. A gun room at the stern end of the gun deck held the ship's weapons, gunpowder, and cannon shot.

Below the gun deck was the cargo hold. Here, the crew placed barrels of wine and other goods the ship usually carried from port to port. The cargo hold extended beneath the waterline. For this reason, the place was wet and damp, often filling with water that sloshed through leaks in the hull. The crew used hand-operated pumps to remove the water when needed. They could also seal the leaks with hot tar.

At the front of the ship was the forecastle. This structure, resembling a large wooden shed, was built atop the main deck. The forecastle provided sleeping quarters for the common sailors. The cook prepared and served meals here as well. From the forecastle, a crew member could reach the gun deck through a hatch in the floor.

A capstan room rose amidships, or in the middle of the ship. The capstan was a stout wooden column used to lift heavy loads, such as barrels, into and out of the cargo hold.

Diagram of the Mayflower

Mizzenmast

Mainmast

On the Deck
View of the deck of the *Mayflower II*

Gun Deck

Foremast

Bowsprit

Below Deck

The *Mayflower II* shows the dark and cramped conditions within the ship.

21

Sailors worked the device by pushing on wooden levers that fit into holes at the top of the capstan. The levers turned the capstan, winding or unwinding chains tied around the barrels. The crew also used the capstan to raise and lower the ship's anchor.

Astern of, or behind, the capstan was steerage. In this small room, the helmsman steered the ship. Because the helmsman's station was below the main deck, he could not see where the ship was going. Orders to turn the ship to port or to starboard were given by a ship's mate standing above the steerage room on the main deck.

A cabin astern of the steerage room provided quarters for the ship's mates, who may have also used the steerage room for sleeping. Another cabin in this part of the ship was for the master's use. The rising deck at the stern of the *Mayflower* was the place for the poop house, where Jones and higher ranking crew would stay. This was the *Mayflower*'s office, where charts (maps) were stored and the master and mates could plot their course.

The Mayflower Partners

England's trade with France in wine and other goods dates back to the Middle Ages (c. 500 to c. 1500), when the southwestern French region of Aquitaine belonged to the kings of England. The wine-growing region around Bordeaux, located in Aquitaine, exported its fine red wines—known in England as claret—to a demanding English market. Aquitaine became French territory after the end of the Hundred Years' War (1337–1453).

The traditional method for transporting wine was to send a huge fleet of hundreds of merchant ships to the city of Bordeaux at Easter and Christmas. The ships carried English goods, including wool and corn, to exchange for barrels of wine, as well as salt and armor. By the 1600s, groups of investors were sending smaller expeditions to Bordeaux and other French ports. The *Mayflower* was one of many similar vessels that were used for this trade.

In approximately 1607, four business partners purchased the *Mayflower*. One of them, Jones, was an experienced sailor and a resident of Harwich. The partners agreed to make Jones the master of the ship. His job was to command the ship on its trading voyages. Jones's title was *master* because the title of *captain* was reserved for military shipmasters and not used on merchant vessels.

Tuns and Tons

The wine trade was so important to English merchant ships that the wine tun, or barrel, became a common unit of measurement. A wine tun held 252 gallons (954 L) of wine, while the smaller hogshead cask held 63 gallons (238 L), or one-fourth of a tun. The tun became the basis for the ton—a weight measurement of 2,000 pounds (907 kg).[4]

The first written record of the *Mayflower* dates from 1609. In that year, a London merchant named Andrew Pawling chartered, or rented, the *Mayflower* for a trading voyage to Norway. He agreed to pay 125 pounds ($28,000 today) to use the ship.[5] He would also have to pay a demurrage, which was a fee for every day the ship remained in port with Pawling's goods on board.

A Sweet Ship

Because it often carried wine, the *Mayflower* was known as a "sweet ship."[6] Such a vessel avoided the foul smells and unsanitary conditions caused by other cargoes, such as livestock. That may be why the *Mayflower* was chosen to carry the Pilgrims across the Atlantic. Sailors of the time believed sweet ships helped passengers resist disease and allowed sailors to more easily survive long voyages.

For the charter fee, the *Mayflower* would bring back Pawling's fish, lumber, and tar to sell in England. Such a voyage could be completed in a short time, as long as fair weather held. But the voyage also took the *Mayflower* through the hazardous waters of the North Sea.

The *Mayflower* was not built to handle long, rough ocean voyages. The high structures on the deck made it hard to sail in a contrary wind. On the return trip, the ship ran into a heavy storm. To lighten the vessel, Jones ordered the crew to throw some of its cargo overboard.

Christopher Jones ⚓

Part Owner and Master of the *Mayflower*

Christopher Jones was a mariner from Harwich. In 1593, he married Sara Twitt. Her father, a shipowner, left her money and a partial ownership in his ship, the *Apollo*, upon his death. After Sara's death at the age of 27 in 1603, Jones married Josian Gray, a widow with homes and property in Harwich. In approximately 1610, Jones moved to Rotherhithe, a town on the south bank of the Thames River, near London.

Before moving to Rotherhithe, in approximately 1607, Jones purchased the *Mayflower* with three partners. As a partner, he had the right to a share of income from the ship's trading voyages and the commissions charged for carrying the Separatists to North America.

History has forgotten the names of most English sea captains, but Jones's fame endures as the master who brought the Pilgrims safely across the stormy Atlantic to the New World. His two-story, whitewashed house still stands on Kings Head Street, in the medieval center of Harwich.

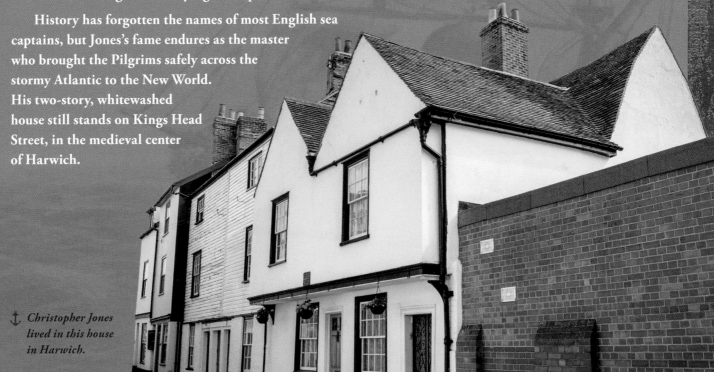

⚓ *Christopher Jones lived in this house in Harwich.*

This may have prevented the ship from sinking, an event that would have probably meant death by drowning for Jones and his crew.

Jones managed to return from Norway with the remaining cargo of 3,000 deals, which are sawn wooden planks, still aboard, as well as tar and herring.[7] Just before Christmas 1609, the *Mayflower* was at its berth in the port of London. In the meantime, officials arrested and jailed Pawling for unpaid debts. Officers of the crown boarded the *Mayflower* and claimed Pawling's goods.

Pawling and the *Mayflower* partners had a legal dispute. To pay some of his debt, Pawling had agreed to turn over his goods to Richard Nottingham. Pawling then sued for the loss of his goods, holding Jones, as master of the ship, responsible. At this point, a record of the ship's goods was needed. This record is the first document in history describing the *Mayflower*. The case with Pawling was tied up in the maritime courts for several years. However, the *Mayflower* was available for use.

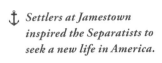
⚓ *Settlers at Jamestown inspired the Separatists to seek a new life in America.*

THE PILGRIMS

Under the reign of King James I (1603–1625), England was expanding its foreign trade and building colonies. At approximately the same time Jones and his partners purchased the *Mayflower*, the first of these colonies in North America began at Jamestown (located near present-day Williamsburg, Virginia). Financed by the Virginia Company, the Jamestown colonists built a small settlement at the mouth of the James River. Most of them died during the next few years as a result of disease and fighting with local Native Americans, but the struggling colony survived.

In the 1600s, North America was a risky place to settle or invest. Despite the troubles and risks, it remained a place of hope for those

Jamestown

The Virginia Company sponsored the first English settlement to survive in North America. This voyage brought a group of men and boys to Virginia in 1607. Their voyage may have served as a lesson for Jones of the *Mayflower* as well as the Pilgrims.

Setting out from England in the dead of winter, the travelers took six weeks to clear the English Channel and then took a southerly route to resupply at the Canary Islands and at several islands in the Caribbean Sea.[1] The route was 6,000 miles (9,700 km), twice as long as the northerly route. The voyage to North America took 144 days.[2]

Once in Virginia, the settlers raised a three-sided stockade and named it Jamestown. Within three years, more than half of them died from disease. Algonquin people who lived in the area also resisted colonization, mounting deadly attacks to protect their lands. Unlike the Separatists, the men who settled Jamestown had little to no experience with farming or raising animals. They were adventurers, and their lack of experience and skills made them ill equipped to settle a colony. The situation improved under the leadership of John Smith. However, he returned to England. Many of those who survived wanted to return to England as well, but their new leader forced them to stay. Jamestown was the capital of the Virginia Colony until almost 1700. Today, the National Park Service manages the colony's site.

who wished to escape England. This included the Separatists, many of whom came from the village of Scrooby, located in northern England. They formed a congregation under two reverends, Richard Clyfton and John Robinson. Seeing the Church of England as a hopelessly corrupt institution, these Christians separated themselves from the official church entirely.

It was an act that made them outlaws. To avoid arrest and imprisonment, they resolved to flee England for a safer place: the Netherlands.

The Separatists first attempted their escape in 1607, when they set out for the Dutch city of Amsterdam. Before their vessel could get underway, the British ship's captain betrayed them. Their possessions were seized, and they were imprisoned in England for a short time.

The next year, they made a second attempt, this time employing a Dutch ship and captain. Spying a group of English soldiers on shore, the captain weighed anchor and fled to the open sea, stranding a group of Separatists on the English shore. This group was imprisoned. By this time, however, they had sold their property and had nothing the king of England could seize. They were released and eventually made their way to Leiden, a bustling factory city in the Netherlands, in 1609.

The Emden Separatists

The Leiden Separatists were not the first English dissenters to set out for the New World from the Netherlands. In the winter of 1619, a group of 180 Separatists left their home in Emden.[3] Their ship reached its destination in Virginia after a rough trip. "They were packed together like herrings," reported Robert Cushman, a leader of the Leiden Separatists. "They had amongst them the flux [dysentery], and also want of fresh water, so as it is here rather wondered at that so many are alive, than so many are dead."[4] Only 50 of the 180 Emden passengers survived the crossing.[5]

Seeking New Refuge

Although they lived in Leiden for more than ten years, the Separatists did not find life easier in the Netherlands than it was in England. They found themselves at odds with the Dutch regarding their religious practices. Many of the Separatists, as country people, also had problems adapting to the crowded city. They were farmers who could barely support themselves by working in Leiden's textile factories. And the Netherlands remained under a threat of invasion by Spain, a Catholic nation that was a sworn enemy to Protestants of all sects, including Separatists.

In approximately 1619, the Separatists made a difficult decision. Some among them would leave Leiden and move to North America. Hearing of their intentions, the Dutch government made them an offer. The Dutch were interested in establishing their own colonies in North America to compete with the English. The government offered to sponsor the Separatists in settling a Dutch colony. The Separatists declined this offer. They were natives of England and wished to remain English citizens.

The Leiden Separatists applied to the Virginia Company for permission to settle in the English colony. Virginia was still under the authority of King James I, but the Separatists

⚓ *Separatist leader John Robinson lived in this house in Leiden.*

believed the king's rule would lay easier on his subjects in a new, distant land. They would be free to follow their own religious beliefs and worship as they pleased.

The king, in turn, wanted to develop the colony. The crown needed settlers to work the land and produce tobacco and other goods. England was a small island with limited resources. Building colonies was important to its trade and its future well-being.

The king also may have wanted to rid himself of the troublesome Separatists. They threatened the church's authority and that of the English courts and government. He agreed to allow Separatists to create a settlement in the New World. However, as head of the Church of England, the king did not want to show the Separatists any favor. He would not acknowledge the agreement publicly.

The Merchant Adventurers

To get to Virginia, the Separatists needed a ship. They also needed money. In the early 1600s, no ships were offering passenger service to North America. That meant the group had to charter a vessel and a crew to sail across 3,000 miles (4,800 km) of ocean.[6] They would need supplies of food, tools, and weapons. It was an expensive proposition.

They sought out Thomas Weston, a London shipowner and investor who had sent trading and fishing vessels to North America. Weston saw the Separatists as promising clients. He was one of a group of approximately 70 investors known as the Merchant Adventurers.[7] Their goal was to establish trading enterprises in North America. The group also intended to spread Christianity to the Native Americans there.

⚓ *The Virginia Company's*
seal included an image
of King James I.

The Virginia Company granted a patent to the Merchant Adventurers. The patent gave
permission to the group to build a new settlement around the mouth of the Hudson River. This
was the northern border of the Virginia colony.

The Merchant Adventurers, in turn, made an agreement with the Separatists, who could
buy shares in the new colony. This made them partners in a joint-stock venture, with an interest

The Journey Was Just Business

Why Jones and his partners, who had always limited the *Mayflower* to European waters, would agree to send it so far and at such a risk is uncertain. The answer may lie in the decline of the English economy in the early 1600s. The business of bartering English wool for French wine, salt, and other goods was never an easy way to make money. By 1620, Dutch competition was challenging merchant shipping and the wool trade. Transporting passengers was one alternative for Jones, who was a practical businessman, not a religious idealist or a promoter of colonization—and certainly not an adventurer.

in seeing the trading business of the colony succeed. The settlers could invest their own money and buy more shares in the venture if they were able. After seven years, the goods of the colony would be divided among all of the shareholders. As part of the deal, the Separatists would have to produce goods for export from North America.

A Routine Voyage

In May 1620, the *Mayflower* set sail from London for the English Channel, hired by the London merchant William Speight. The channel separates the island of Great Britain from the European continent. Safe harbors at Southampton, Bournemouth, and Plymouth offer shelter during storms. But the prevailing westerly winds can make sailing difficult, even on a clear day. Jones, like others on this course, may have ordered the ship to make frequent, zigzagging turns as his ship beat against the wind. It could take weeks or even months for a vessel under sail to get out of the channel and reach the vast open seas of the North Atlantic Ocean.

The *Mayflower* headed west and then southwest, around the peninsula of Brittany, France. Turning southeast, it crossed the Bay of Biscay and made port at La Rochelle, on the west coast of France. Since the 1100s, trade in wine and other goods had brought many English ships to La Rochelle's spacious harbor.

Upon returning to the docks of London, the crew of the *Mayflower* unloaded Speight's valuable cargo: 59 tuns and one hogshead of wine.[8] This was much less than what the *Mayflower* could hold at full capacity. The crew may have unloaded other tuns at Southampton before the ship reached London.

There was nothing unusual in this two-month voyage. In the spring of 1620, the *Mayflower* was an ordinary ship, earning money by transporting goods between England and the European continent. The partners charged fees to English merchants for the voyage and also earned money by selling English goods abroad. But that summer, Jones and his partners would agree to a very different enterprise for their vessel.

Chapter 4

PREPARING TO SAIL

The Separatists tasked Weston with getting a ship for their voyage. He dallied for several months. While waiting for Weston to procure a vessel, the group decided to purchase a second, smaller ship that would remain with them in North America.

The Speedwell

In June 1620, the Separatists bought the *Speedwell* in the Netherlands. The *Speedwell* was a pinnace, a lighter and smaller ship

⚓ *The* Mayflower II *displays some of the foods the Pilgrims ate. Biscuits were baked twice to dry them out so they would not spoil.*

than the *Mayflower*. Under favorable conditions, the *Speedwell* could manage a transatlantic voyage. But it would prove useful at the Pilgrims' destination as well.

The ship's small size made it ideal for fishing in and exploring North American rivers such as the Hudson. The ship would also allow members of the colony to travel up and down the North American coast in relative safety.

Gathering Supplies

At approximately the time the Separatists bought the *Speedwell*, one of the London investors drew up a list of suggested provisions for the voyage. Food items included biscuits, salt pork, peas, oats, wheat, butter, oil, cod, cheese vinegar, rice, bacon, and cider. The Separatists were also advised to bring beer, which kept better than water. Beer had just enough alcohol to kill any microbes, though people did not know that at the time.

The list also included cooking items and dishware. Each household should have an iron cooking pot, skillets, dishes, and a frying pan. And the colonists would need a store of armor, swords, and gunpowder for hunting and self-defense. As for tools, they should bring hoes, a broad axe, a handsaw, hammers, shovels, chisels, hatchets, nails, locks, and a grinding stone to sharpen blades.

Cooking on the Mayflower

The *Mayflower*'s crew and passengers had only a tiny galley space to serve as their kitchen. Using frying pans, a griddle, and a large iron kettle set up on a tripod, the cook prepared the meals. For heat, he built a fire using a small hearth box filled with sand. The smoke vented out of an opening in the deck.

An open fire aboard a wooden ship was dangerous, especially when the sea was rough. The portable hearth box could be moved in fair weather to the main deck, where there was less likelihood of a serious fire breaking out.

Weston Hires the Mayflower

As the Separatists prepared for their trip to the New World, Weston finally made progress on chartering a vessel. Through his contacts in the port of London, Weston learned of the *Mayflower*. He hired the ship from Jones and his partners. Jones was an experienced shipmaster, and his two pilots, Robert Coppin and John Clarke, had already been to North America.

Jones hired a surgeon to look after the health of the crew and passengers. Jones also hired a cooper to look after the water and food barrels. In all, approximately 30 crew members and mates were needed to sail the *Mayflower*.[1] The ship was usually anchored in the sprawling port of London, among the bustling docks and wharves. Its master, mates, and crew members lived nearby. After preparing the crew and the ship, Jones sailed it to the English Channel port of Southampton, the designated meeting point. He traveled there with passengers. Weston had also hired laborers and skilled workers to help build the colony in North America. These hired hands were non-Separatists. They were the Strangers.

Meanwhile, the Separatists met in July to discuss their future. When first planning the voyage, they decided to send 150 of their members to the New World.[2] But some of the congregation could not ready themselves in time, nor did they have the financial means to go, and so they had to stay behind. On July 31, 1620, the Separatists who would make the voyage

⚓ *An early map of Cape Cod shows Clark's Island.*

Map of
PLYMOUTH BAY
Scale 2½ Miles per Inch

N

DUXBURY

DUXBURY BEACH

Capt and Hill

Kingston Bay

Clark's Island

Garnet

Saquish Head

Pier

RAIL ROAD

High Cliffs

HARBOR

BEACH

Rock

PLYMOUTH

MANOMET

Billington Sea

John Clarke ⚓

Pilot of the *Mayflower*

Before the voyage of the *Mayflower*, Christopher Jones had never been to North America. It was uncommon for English shipmasters to make this long, risky voyage unless they were trading directly with Jamestown, the settlement established by the Virginia colonists. Perhaps for that reason, Jones and his partners hired John Clarke as their pilot.

Clarke had long experience sailing the coasts of North America. He had served as a ship's pilot on a voyage to Jamestown in 1611. But his time in Virginia was cut short by a Spanish raiding party. Enemies of the English, the Spanish took Clarke prisoner and brought him back to Spain. Clarke was imprisoned there for five years. The experience did not stop him from a return voyage to Jamestown in 1618 or from agreeing to pilot the *Mayflower* in 1620.

Clarke's skill as a boat pilot brought a party of *Mayflower* passengers and crew safely ashore on a sandy islet during a stormy winter's night in Cape Cod Bay. His feat inspired the party to name Clark's Island in Plymouth Bay for him.

moved from Leiden to Delfshaven, a Dutch port. The *Speedwell* was there, ready for its voyage to North America.

The trip to North America would be no ordinary journey for either vessel. The *Mayflower* had been transporting cargo between England and the continent of Europe for more than ten years. Ordinarily, the *Speedwell* carried goods for English merchants. But instead of cargo, the *Mayflower* and the *Speedwell* would carry 120 passengers, approximately 90 on the *Mayflower* and approximately 30 on the *Speedwell*.[3] The men, women, children, servants, and pets taking shelter below their decks were venturing to a new life in a distant, strange, and dangerous land.

Setting Off

The *Speedwell*, with Master Reynolds commanding, set out from Delfshaven. Reynolds's first name is lost to history. While the passengers settled into dark, cramped cargo holds, the *Speedwell* joined the *Mayflower* in Southampton. The master of the *Speedwell* had ordered

The Separatists Celebrate

The Separatists held a farewell feast. One member, Edward Winslow, wrote later about the celebration: "We refreshed ourselves, after our tears, with singing of Psalms, making joyful melody in our hearts as well as with the voice, there being many of the Congregation very expert in music; and indeed it was the sweetest melody that ever mine ears heard."[4]

repairs on his ship before heading to the open seas. It seemed the boat was taking on water, and repairs were needed, as the smallest leak on a 3,000-mile (4,800 km) ocean voyage could mean disaster.

There was no mystery, at least to Master Reynolds, about the problem. In Delfshaven, he had outfitted the *Speedwell* with a larger mast. A larger mast meant more sail area to move the boat, but it also meant more strain on the wooden planks that made up the ship's hull. As the planks separated under the strain, a slow leak started that threatened to gradually swamp the vessel.

Reynolds knew he could stop the leak simply by setting a smaller area of sail on the mast. Fewer sails catching the wind would reduce the strain on the hull. But the leak also meant Reynolds could declare the ship unseaworthy. He could then turn back to England and end the *Speedwell*'s voyage to North America. Nobody would question him. The master of a civilian ship had absolute authority over the actions of that ship at sea.

On August 5, 1620, the *Speedwell* and the *Mayflower* set out from Southampton. While still cruising along the southern English coast, the *Speedwell* began taking on water. The two ships sailed into the port of Dartmouth, in the English region of Cornwall. There, the crew of the *Speedwell* again tried to patch the vessel for the long voyage to North America. Upon leaving

Dartmouth, on approximately August 21, the ship began to take on water again. The two vessels took shelter at Plymouth, waited another two weeks, and set out again on September 6.

Life on the Gun Deck

The *Mayflower* was not outfitted for passengers. The Pilgrims slept on the gun deck, directly below the main deck. The gun deck was uncomfortable. The ceiling was low, measuring approximately 6 feet (2 m) high, making it difficult for some passengers to stand up and walk around.[5] Where the beams supporting the upper deck crossed, the headroom was even less. There was little air, no light after sundown, and no privacy. For 66 days, the Pilgrims lived a miserable existence at sea, and many would have to remain on the ship for weeks after the ship reached land.[6]

Point of No Return

For the crew of any ship, a voyage to North America inspired fear. It was not simply the danger of an ocean crossing. Starvation, disease, freezing winter temperatures, and potentially hostile native peoples also threatened their survival. The masters and crews of the *Mayflower* and the *Speedwell* were to wait for the next fair sailing weather, in the spring of 1621, to return to England. But they did not have enough supplies on board the ships to survive a long winter.

These facts unsettled the master and crew of the *Speedwell*. They were risking their lives for little reward. They had no rights to land or property in the New World, as did the settlers lodged in their ship. They also knew the *Mayflower* was carrying most of the provisions for the voyage. Should the ships become separated, the passengers and crew of the *Speedwell* would starve first. Reynolds may have thought the pay was not worth such risk.

Approximately 300 miles (480 km) into their journey, the *Speedwell* sprang another leak.[7] It was a crucial point of no return. The ship had to turn back or press on and make the crossing in the heavy late-fall weather while taking on water.

Reynolds and Jones agreed to part ways. Some of the *Speedwell*'s passengers climbed aboard the *Mayflower* with their belongings and moved into the ship's crowded gun deck. Almost 20 passengers remained on the *Speedwell*, which returned to a safe harbor in England.[8] With a fair wind and a crowded hold, the *Mayflower* proceeded west to North America.

Chapter 5

THE MAYFLOWER AT SEA

The *Mayflower* rolled across the North Atlantic, tracking westward for North America. Jones had experience with long sea voyages. As master of the *Mayflower*, he had weathered heavy storms and guided the ship along dangerous coasts. But this was the first time Jones and his ship would risk the 3,000-mile (4,800 km) Atlantic crossing.

Jones and the crew of the *Mayflower* lived and worked according to the old routines of a seaborne vessel. Their day was divided into watches of four hours. A crewman or mate on watch had to stand at attention on deck and be ready to carry out orders instantly. He had to watch the sea and the horizon for signs of unfavorable weather, dangerous waves, and ships—friendly or unfriendly.

At all times, the ship's rudder was under the control of a helmsman. He stood in the steering compartment, located at the back of the ship, directly below the quarterdeck. He kept the ship on track by gripping a whipstaff, which was a vertical pole. Moving the whipstaff to the left or right controlled the ship's course. A gap in the deck and another in the hull below it allowed the whipstaff to be linked directly to the tiller, which connects to the rudder via a rudder post.

Midnight at Sea

All ships had to keep time. Although clocks existed at the time of the *Mayflower*'s voyage, they were rare, expensive, and inaccurate. To keep time, most ships used a sandglass, turned every half hour. A few hours after sunset, and if the weather was clear, one of the mates brought out the nocturnal. This round, metal device had several metal disks and a hole set in the middle. A nocturnal made use of Polaris, the North Star.

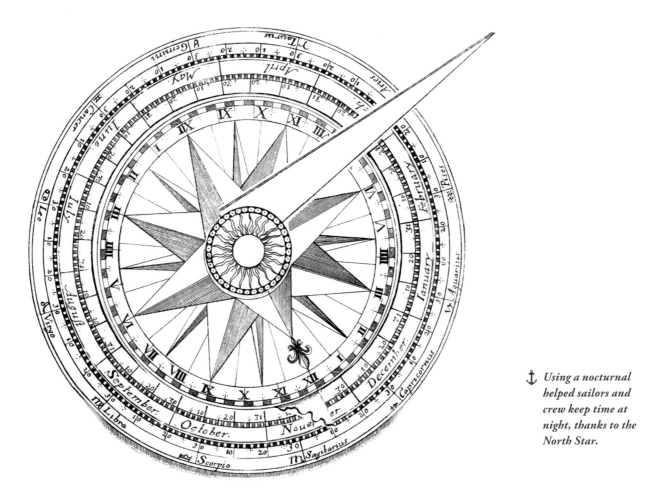

⚓ *Using a nocturnal helped sailors and crew keep time at night, thanks to the North Star.*

Polaris has been a dependable guide for mariners since ancient times. It lies directly over the axis of Earth's rotation. It appears fixed in the sky while the other stars rotate around it. The position of these stars with respect to Polaris and the position of Polaris itself give clues to the time of day and the direction of the ship.

The Sailor's Life

The crew of the *Mayflower* did not enjoy much more comfort than the passengers enjoyed. Sailors slept on deck in fair weather. In rainy or cold conditions, they used hammocks in the forecastle, in the front of the ship, or in a cabin astern. The accommodations were spare. Waves crashing over the ship's bow and deck constantly leaked into their sleeping quarters, making it damp and cold.

On deck, handling slippery hempen ropes was difficult. The fiber hardened when wet, making it tougher to grip. And from time to time, even an experienced sailor fell to the deck. Going over the side in the North Atlantic Ocean usually meant a quick, cold death by drowning.

While sighting Polaris through the nocturnal's central hole, the mate moved a thin lever on the device until the lever pointed to two bright stars in the sky. A mark on the nocturnal directly underneath the arm of the lever then showed the time. When the nocturnal showed midnight, the sandglass was turned, marking the beginning of the midnight watch.

Mayflower *Technology*

The master and his mates had several other instruments aboard. To show direction, the ship relied on a compass. This was a small, circular card set inside a wooden box placed directly in front of the helmsman to help him keep the ship on track. The card pivoted on a long, thin piece of magnetized iron. As the ship pitched and rolled, the compass sat quietly, perched on a set of brass gimbals, or supports. The gimbals kept the compass as level and steady as possible while allowing it to rotate as the ship's direction changed.

⚓ *The compass was an invaluable tool in navigating the* Mayflower *from England to North America.*

The compass card showed 32 points that indicated direction, including the four cardinal points of north, south, east, and west. As the ship's directions changed, the compass card also turned. Earth's magnetic field acted on the iron, turning the compass card to indicate the direction of the magnetic North Pole. Relying on the compass, Jones and his mates could keep the ship moving in a slightly south of west direction, which they knew would eventually bring them to the eastern coast of North America.

The crew used a traverse board to more precisely track the ship's course. This device was helpful because the *Mayflower*—and all other ships under sail—could not move in a straight line for long distances. Instead, as the wind changed direction, these vessels had to tack, or change course, to catch a favorable following breeze. If the wind began blowing directly against the ship, the master had to turn to port or starboard and adjust the sails to start moving again.

The traverse board used a circular series of small peg holes around its edge, showing the 32 points of the compass. It also had long rows of eight small holes set along each radius of the 32 points. After each turn of the half-hour sandglass, the helmsman placed a peg in the row corresponding to the ship's heading. He also marked the direction on a slate. At the end of the watch, Jones or one of his mates used this record of the ship's headings. They could then chart the *Mayflower*'s approximate course from the last four hours.

Finally, the master had to gauge the speed of his ship. Speedometers did not exist. Instead, mariners of the *Mayflower*'s time used a chip log. This was a line of rope with a quarter-circle of wood attached at one end. The line was set into the water and allowed to run out as the ship moved forward. Knots were tied into the line at intervals. Using a fast sandglass, which ran out

⚓ *A traverse board was essential to navigators on the Mayflower and other ships.*

John Smith and New England

In 1616, John Smith, one of the leaders of the Virginia Colony, published the first English map of the part of North America known today as New England. Two years earlier, Smith had explored more than 300 miles (480 km) of coastline with several companions in a small boat. Eager to have the English settle this remote region, he named it New England.

Smith was an enthusiastic promoter of North America, which he believed would return high profits to anyone brave enough to settle there. After returning to England, he advertised the promise of this new land in the book *A Description of New England*. Smith wrote about fertile lands and abundant wildlife. Plymouth, he claimed, had "an excellent good harbor, good land; and no want of any thing, but industrious people."[2] The Leiden Separatists purchased a copy of Smith's map, and Jones may have had this copy aboard the *Mayflower*.

in less than a minute, and counting how many knots were reeled out gave a rough measure of the ship's speed counted in nautical miles—or knots—per hour. The knot is still used as a measure of speed at sea: one knot equals 1.15 miles (1.85 km) per hour.[1]

Finding Virginia

Using a compass, a traverse board, and a chip log, a navigator in the early 1600s could plot the day-to-day course on the North Atlantic Ocean on a sea chart. But the marks made on a chart still represented only a guess regarding the ship's position. To have a better idea of exactly where they were, Jones and his mates used an astrolabe.

This instrument showed the height above the horizon of certain stars, which in turn showed the ship's latitude above the equator. The latitude of important landmarks was already known and shown on the charts that were essential to navigation.

London lay at latitude 51.5 degrees north, for example, and the colony settlement at Jamestown, Virginia, was at 37.2 degrees north. In theory, the *Mayflower* simply had to reach the latitude of Virginia and sail directly west to reach its destination. John Smith and other Virginia colonists had already charted this coastal region, with its many river mouths, sandbars, shoals, and inlets. Jones may have had those charts available and planned to use them once he sighted land. But even though Virginia was their destination, Jones, his crew, and the passengers of the *Mayflower* would never see it.

⚓ *Winter storms toss the seas
off Cape Cod.*

REACHING CAPE COD

ven in fair weather, sailing in the North Atlantic can be rough. Prevailing winds blow from the west, churning the sea. Large vessels pitch and roll in the waves. Smaller ships are tossed like corks.

The passengers on the *Mayflower* had only a few feet of space to sleep. There were no chairs or beds, and even standing up on the low-ceilinged gun deck could be difficult. It was early fall, the air was growing cold, and the passengers' clothes were growing filthy. The ship had no bathroom, shower, or running water. Animals were on

Chapter 6

board, too, including goats, dogs, and sheep. With so little room, the constant roll of the ship, and no proper beds, it was difficult to sleep.

Seasickness affected many of the passengers. The constant motion of a ship causes the body to lose its sense of balance. The results are dizziness, nausea, and vomiting. The crowding and lack of fresh air on the *Mayflower* made the uncomfortable symptoms worse. Crew members, who had spent much of their lives at sea, went about their tasks without feeling any ill effects.

A Troublesome Sailor

Working on the main deck, the crew could not worry about the passengers below. But one crew member went out of his way to hurl nasty insults and threats their way. Separatist William Bradford wrote about this troublesome sailor:

> *There was a proud and very profane young man; one of the sea-men, of a lusty, able body, which made him the more haughty; he would always be condemning the poor people in their sickness, and cursing them daily with grievous execrations, and told them, that he hoped to help to cast half of them over board before they came to their journey's end, and to make merry with what they had; and if he were by any gently reproved, he would curse and swear most bitterly.[1]*

The passengers could do nothing to stop the sailor's cruel mockery. In their view, God would provide for their safety and the success of the voyage.

One day, the sailor came down with an illness. He soon died. His was the first death of the *Mayflower*'s voyage, and his body was the first to be cast into the sea. The passengers saw this event as a sign from God. They believed the illness was divine vengeance for the sailor's poor treatment of them.

Time of Danger

With a shallow draft and spacious cargo hold, the *Mayflower* was built for coastal trading voyages. Ocean sailing posed different challenges, especially when sailing against the wind. The pear-shaped profile of the ship, lying wide and squat in the water, made it difficult to sail close-hauled, or with the wind blowing from ahead. Progress was slow, often only a few miles

A Near-Death Experience

The main deck of the *Mayflower* allowed the passengers fresh air and sunshine when the weather was clear. But it also held dangers. William Bradford described how someone was thrown overboard. His description, paraphrased in more modern English says, "In a mighty storm, a strapping young man (called John Howland) was, with a lurch of the ship thrown into the sea; but it pleased God that he caught hold of the ropes which hung overboard. He held his hold (though he was many feet under water) till he was hauled up by the same rope to the brim of the water, and then with a boathook and other means got into the ship again, and his life saved."[2]

William **Bradford**

Separatist and Pilgrim

Born in 1590 in Yorkshire, William Bradford joined the Separatists while he was still a teenager. In 1609, he fled with the group to Leiden. He became a leader of the Separatists who resolved to make the risky journey to North America. Bradford and his wife, Dorothy, left a four-year-old son behind. Shortly after their arrival off Cape Cod, Bradford's wife fell from the deck of the *Mayflower* and drowned. Bradford married a widowed woman, Alice Carpenter Southworth, around 1623. The couple raised her two sons, Bradford's son (who came over from Leiden), and three children they had together.

The Separatists unanimously elected Bradford as the governor of Plymouth in 1621, following the death of their first governor, John Carver. Bradford remained the colony's elected governor until his death in 1657. He kept a diary as well as important records of the voyage, including a copy of the original Mayflower Compact. Bradford also wrote a history of the colony, *Of Plymouth Plantation*, that has remained a vital source of information for historians.

in a day. If a storm came up, the crew had to take in or tie up the sails because having sails set out in a storm made it more difficult to control the ship. Heavy winds could rip and shred the unfurled canvas sails, while the strain on the masts could snap them from their moorings in the ship's hull. In heavy weather, with the sails furled and the rudder almost useless for controlling the ship, the *Mayflower* could easily drift off course.

As the weeks passed, the weather grew worse. Heavy storms battered the ship. Waves crashed over the rails and flooded the decks. The ship started taking on water. The constant strain cracked one of the ship's main beams. The officers and crew had no equipment available to repair it. In time, with the constant strain, the crack would grow. The beam might split in two, and the ship might start coming apart.

Jones and his officers talked among themselves. They had a difficult decision. The ship's carpenter had no tools to repair the beam. There were no harbors or ports nearby where they could go for safety and to make the repair. And in this ocean expanse, halfway to their destination, turning back would be just as risky as going ahead.

On talking with the passengers, the crew of the *Mayflower* discovered the colonists had brought several heavy tools. They had intended to use this equipment to build their homes and farms in the New World. Among their store of equipment was a large iron screw jack.

A Screwy Mystery

The Pilgrims' large iron screw jack, as mentioned by Bradford, poses a riddle to historians. They agree the tool was used at sea to support the ship's cracked main beam. What they do not know is why the group would bring this heavy tool with them when space on the ship was so limited. To this day, the intended purpose of the tool remains a mystery.

A screw could serve as a jack or support underneath heavy roof beams and is useful when a house is under construction. Another possibility is that the screw jack was part of a printing press used to create religious pamphlets. In the early printing process, paper was pressed against wooden type to create a book or pamphlet page. If the Pilgrims had a printing press, they also had good cause to hide it and to be coy about describing it. Printing in England could be dangerous. Religious dissenters could be arrested, imprisoned, or executed for writing against the king or the Church of England.

It may have been part of a printing press. The carpenter examined the tool and spoke with Jones. It might serve their purpose. They dragged the screw jack from the storage hold and placed it underneath the cracked beam. They gradually raised the screw to shore up the beam, placing a post underneath for support. The cracked beam held fast.

The heavy seas continued. Winds blew against the ship. Several times, the *Mayflower* was forced to heave to, or position the sails parallel to the wind. This prevented damage to the sails and mast. It also helped to stabilize the vessel, making the ride more pleasant. The ship would travel a bit in the direction the wind was blowing, but not as far as it would if the wind were blowing into the sails.

Arrival

On November 9, after more than 60 days at sea, the *Mayflower* came within sight of land.[3] But Jones had missed Virginia by a considerable distance. Instead of a lush forest lining the banks of a wide river, he saw a flat beach and sandy, wooded cliffs. He had brought the ship to the windswept coast of Cape Cod, which juts into the Atlantic Ocean like a large, flexing arm from the New England coast.

This narrow peninsula was well known to English fishing vessels. For many years, they had been sailing there in search of whales and the abundant fish for which the peninsula was named. Behind the cape, to the west, was a wide bay with several suitable harbors. There were no European settlements this far north, but Native Americans lived and hunted in the region.

The Pilgrims did not have a charter to settle there. They had been granted land much farther south along the Hudson River. But the travelers had only a simple chart of the coastal region to aid them on their way.

From the deck of the *Mayflower*, the passengers gazed at the strange land. They were relieved at their survival. They were also uncertain of what to do next.

THE PORTRAICTUER OF CAPTAINE IOHN SMITH ADMIRALL OF NEW ENGLAND.

Æ ta 37
Aᵒ 1616

These are the Lines that shew thy Face; but those
That shew thy Grace and Glory, brighter bee:
Thy Faire-Discoueries and Fowle-Overthrowes
Of Salvages, much Civiliz'd by thee
Best shew thy Spirit; and to it Glory Wyn;
So, thou art Brasse without, but Golde within.

If so; in Brasse (two soft Smiths Acts to beare)
I fix thy Fame, to make Brasse Steele out weare.
Thine as thou art Virtues.
John Dauies. Heref:

NEW ENGLAND

The most remarqueable parts thus named.
by the high and mighty Prince CHARLES,
Prince of great Britaine

HONY SOIT QVI MAL I PENSE

Edenborough

Cambridg
The Base

Schooters hill

Sandwich

Dartmouth

Snadoun hill

Ipswich

Bostou

Hull

Poynt Dauies

Smith Iles

SouthHampton

Bristow

Bassable

Fawmouth

Talbotts Bay

Fullerton Ils

The River CHARLES

Cary Ils

Cheuyot hills

P. Murry

London

Cape ANNA

Leth

The River forth

St John Towne

Norwich

Hoghton Ils

Barty Ils

Wil

Kent

Harington Bay

Cape Elizabeth

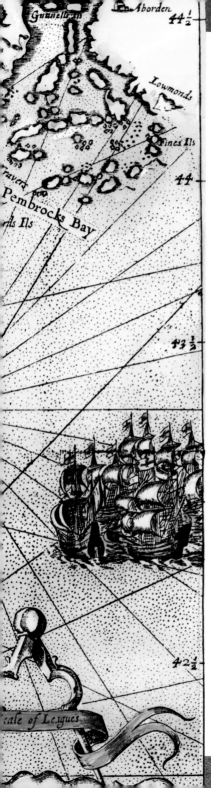

⚓ *John Smith's map of New England could have been a great asset to Jones and his crew on the* Mayflower.

FIRST EXPLORATIONS

J ones had taken the *Mayflower* on a northerly track across the Atlantic Ocean. The distance to North America from England was shorter along this route than on the more southerly track. Also, the many pirates and privateers who infested the Caribbean Sea and coasts of North America avoided these cold, rough waters.

The ship arrived safely after 66 days at sea. The *Mayflower* stood off Cape Cod, its sails lowered and its anchor set. Jones had dozens of sick, hungry, and exhausted passengers aboard. If he did not get them ashore before winter arrived, the *Mayflower* would become a ship of

Mayflower *Births*

The *Mayflower* arrived in North America with an additional passenger. During the voyage across the Atlantic, Elizabeth Hopkins gave birth to a boy. Because the baby was born at sea, Elizabeth and her husband, Stephen, named him Oceanus.

Peregrine White was born soon after the ship's arrival at Cape Cod. *Peregrine* means "traveler." The cradle his parents brought on the *Mayflower* is on display at the Pilgrim Hall Museum in Plymouth, Massachusetts.

Although Oceanus died as a young child, White lived to be 83 years old. White was the subject of the only obituary ever published for a *Mayflower* passenger, printed in the Boston *Newsletter*: "Marshfield, July, 22 Capt. Peregrine White of this Town, Aged Eighty three years, and Eight Months; died the 20th Instant. He was vigorous and of a comly Aspect to the last; Was the Son of Mr. William White and Susanna his Wife; born on board the Mayflower, Capt. Jones Commander, in Cape Cod Harbour, November, 1620. Was the First Englishman born in New-England. Altho' he was in the former part of his Life extravagant; yet was much Reform'd in his last years; and died hopefully."[1]

disease, starvation, and death. There were safe harbors on the other side of the cape, but winds were blowing from the north, making a journey around its tip difficult.

Jones resolved to sail south, with the prevailing winds, to the Hudson River, their original destination. He ordered the *Mayflower* to set sail again. The crew gathered around the capstan, the heavy winch set in the main deck. Leaning into the capstan's levers, they marched in a circle, cranking the device. This raised a heavy chain linked to the anchor. A few turns of the capstan raised the anchor to its resting place in the side of the hull. Setting its sails again, the *Mayflower* got underway and headed south.

The Nantucket Shoals

On a map of the New England coast, the mouth of the Hudson seemed close enough—only 220 miles (350 km) away.[2] With a favorable following breeze, the *Mayflower* could reach the river in a couple days. Navigation would be easy. At first, the ship would be in sight of the steep sand cliffs of Cape Cod and then the New England mainland. Sailors also used easily spotted landmarks: the islands that lay off the cape's southern coast. The Wampanoag, a local Native American people, called them *Natockete* and *Noepe*.[3] Today, they are known as Nantucket Island and Martha's Vineyard. Even with such guideposts, the *Mayflower* faced dangerous sailing.

Jones had two options. He could sail the *Mayflower* between Nantucket and the mainland or take the *Mayflower* around Nantucket. Either way, the ship and its passengers faced danger. Both routes posed the same problem: shallow water.

If the *Mayflower* ran aground, heavy ocean swells would batter the ship. If the crew could not get the ship off the impeding sandbar or rocky ledge, the waves would eventually tear the *Mayflower* to pieces. The *Mayflower* did carry two additional boats, a shallop and a long boat. But the shallop was stowed in several pieces and might take days for the ship's carpenter

Atlantic Ocean

(MASSACHUSETTS)

PLYMOUTH

CAPE COD

NOEPE
(MARTHA'S VINEYARD)

NATOCKETE
(NANTUCKET)

N
W E
S

to reassemble, while the long boat could only carry a few passengers. In the meantime, the passengers and crew would find themselves at the ocean's mercy.

Shifting Winds

With the crew taking constant soundings, the ship made its way along a steep underwater drop-off near the Cape Cod coast. The northerly breeze made for an easy sail. But after leaving the cape, the *Mayflower* had 15 miles (24 km) of open water to cross before reaching sight of Nantucket.[4] There, the breeze died and the water grew shallow.

With the wind starting to drop, Jones and his crew lost control of the ship's direction. He could bark orders to the helmsman, stationed below, gripping the whipstaff that controlled the rudder. But in calmer winds, the strong ocean currents and tides took over. The *Mayflower* risked drifting out of control and heading inland to the shoals. "They fell amongst dangerous shoals and roaring breakers," reported Bradford, "and they were so far entangled therewith as they conceived themselves in great danger."[5]

Late in the afternoon, the wind began to shift. It moved to the east and then to the south. This gave Jones the opportunity to move across the shallow water before the sun went down. The ship would have to set its anchor again, and Jones was not willing to risk sailing such risky waters after dark. The *Mayflower* stood five miles (8 km) off the southeastern tip of Cape Cod.[6] But the shifting winds were blowing against his course for the Hudson River.

Graveyard of Ships

Jones would not be the last sailor to turn his ship to safety after facing the dangerous shoals off Cape Cod. The swirling tides and shallow waters have wrecked more than 1,000 ships since the *Mayflower* dropped anchor. During the heavy winters of the early 1800s, on average, two ships were lost there every month.[7]

Ships of many times and types still lie underwater. Their goods were usually plundered by locals, but most sunken ships could not be salvaged and returned to service. The wreck of the *Frances*, which ran aground off the village of Truro in 1872, can still be seen from the shore at low tide.

Mayflower Compact

Aboard the *Mayflower*, Jones was in command. There was no government, democracy, or voting. He decided where the ship would sail and what dangers it must avoid. After a few hours of very nervous sailing, he decided to return north and land his passengers somewhere on Cape Cod.

The decision caused anger below decks. The Pilgrims argued bitterly among themselves about their future course. The Separatists in the group would obey the decisions of their leaders. Several of the Strangers promised to go their own way after reaching the shore.

The Strangers were not subject to the decisions of the Separatists. They had come as common settlers. They would make their way in the New World as free individuals. The best place to do so was Virginia. They had no interest in living in Cape Cod, left to face Native Americans they assumed to be hostile alongside the members of a strange religious sect.

But Jones would sail no farther. They would have to work together to survive in this new land. Somehow, the Pilgrims must come to an agreement. The Separatists and the Strangers must allow their decisions to be guided by common consent, not by religious beliefs or doctrine about which they would not agree.

On the evening of November 10, 1620, as Jones prepared to return the *Mayflower* north, several of his passengers drafted the Mayflower Compact. In this document, they agreed to "combine ourselves together into a civil body politic" and to "enact, constitute and frame such just and equal laws, ordinances, acts, constitutions and offices, from time to time, as shall be thought most meet and convenient for the general good of the colony, unto which we promise all due submission and obedience."[8] The group came together for the benefit of everyone. This togetherness would prove critical in their success in the New World.

⚓ The Pilgrims negotiated their differences to establish the Mayflower Compact, an agreement for self-governance that later Americans would echo when declaring the colonies free from England.

DELAYING THE RETURN JOURNEY

On November 11, 1620, Jones brought the *Mayflower* to anchor. The ship stood in a natural harbor four miles (6 km) wide.[1] Lying on the northwestern shore of Cape Cod, the harbor was well protected from the tall waves breaking on the other side of the cape.

That morning, 41 men aboard the *Mayflower* signed the Mayflower Compact.[2] In this spot, the king of England would have no direct authority. Nor would the governor

The Mayflower Compact

Using updated English, the Mayflower Compact proclaimed, "IN THE NAME OF GOD, AMEN. We, whose names are underwritten, the Loyal Subjects of our dread Sovereign Lord King *James* . . . covenant and combine ourselves together into a civil Body Politick, for our better Ordering and Preservation, and Furtherance of the Ends aforesaid: And by Virtue hereof do enact, constitute, and frame, such just and equal Laws, Ordinances, Acts, Constitutions, and Officers, from time to time, as shall be thought most meet and convenient for the general Good of the Colony."[3]

Although the original document was lost, Bradford made a copy that was printed in "Mourt's Relation," a pamphlet about the settlement created in London in 1622.

The ideas expressed in the Mayflower Compact would continue with the rebellious British colonists and become part of the foundation of the country they established: the United States of America.

⚓ *The Mayflower Compact was the first constitution in the colonies, outlining how the Plymouth Colony would be governed.*

of Virginia have any say in their laws. Instead, the Pilgrims would form a government among themselves and make their decisions together. Ten days later, they elected John Carver, one of the Separatists, as the first governor.

Jones and the crew of the *Mayflower* had brought the Pilgrims to the New World and fulfilled their agreement. They had not agreed to remain any longer than necessary. There were no items of trade here and nobody to trade with. The ship's stores of food and water were running low. The return voyage to England would be shorter than the voyage to North America because prevailing winds blew from the west, in the direction they would be heading. That would hopefully make for a quick crossing.

be as firme as any patent; and in some respects more sure.
The forme was as followeth.

In y name of god Amen. We whose names are underwriten,
the loyall subjects of our dread soueraigne Lord king James,
by y grace of god, of great Britaine, franc, & Ireland king,
defender of y faith, &c.

Haueing undertaken, for y glorie of god, and aduancemente
of y christian faith and honour of our king & countrie, a voyage to
plant y first colonie in y Northerne parts of Virginia. Doe
by these presents solemnly & mutualy in y presence of god, and
one of another, Couenant, & combine our selues togeather into a
Ciuill body politick; for our better ordering, & preseruation & fur=
therance of y ends aforesaid; and by vertue hearof to Enacte,
constitute, and frame shuch just & equall Lawes, ordinances,
Acts, constitutions, & offices, from time to time, as shall be thought
most meete & conuenient for y generall good of y Colonie: unto
which we promise all due submission and obedience. In witnes
wherof we haue hereunder subscribed our names at Cap=
Codd y .11. of Nouember, in y year of y raigne of our soueraigne
Lord king James of England, franc, & Ireland y eighteenth
and of Scotland y fiftie fourth. An: Dom. 1620.]
After this they chose, or rather confirmed m John caruer (a man
godly & well approued amongst them) their gouernour for that
year. And after they had prouided a place for their goods, or

Going Ashore

But Jones decided to remain in North America, though only temporarily. From the ship, he could see no suitable land for farming or any rivers or other water sources. Leaving the Pilgrims to face the winter alone would probably doom them.

The colonists and the crew had reason to fear the inhabitants. Although only a few of them had ever seen North America, bloody tales of combat between Native groups and the Jamestown Colony were well known in England. In fact, several groups of Algonquian speakers lived in the coastal regions of southern New England. The Nauset made their homes on Cape Cod, and the Patuxet lived farther west, on the mainland around Plymouth. Both of these groups belonged to the Wampanoag confederation, whose leader, Massasoit, ruled from Cape Cod down to what is now Rhode Island.

Jones decided he would help his passengers find a suitable spot for a permanent settlement. His crew would fish, hunt game, and search for water. If necessary, they would defend themselves and the settlers against Native Americans. In fair weather, crew members would carry out any needed repairs to the ship's sails, rigging, and hull. The *Mayflower* would shelter them during winter storms.

To explore this long coast, the group needed the shallop. Its smaller size was better suited to the shallow waters. But the rough voyage had battered the boat. The carpenter announced that it would take several days for him to repair and assemble it. On Sunday, November 12, the Separatists observed the Sabbath. In the following days, they appointed Captain Myles Standish to lead a shore party of 16 men.[4]

Standish was a Stranger and a soldier who had fought for Queen Elizabeth I's army in the Netherlands. There, he met and befriended the Leiden Separatists. Although he never joined the sect, he agreed to sail to North America with them as their military captain.

The Standish party set out in the ship's long boat on November 15. The men landed at what is now the shore of Provincetown harbor and then walked southward along Cape Cod's beaches and sandy, forested hills. They spotted a group of five or six Nauset, who fled into the woods. Following their tracks, the party came across signs of a small village, a

The Legend of Plymouth Rock

According to tradition, the Pilgrims first landed at Plymouth Rock. The first exploring parties went ashore at what is now Provincetown, at the northern tip of Cape Cod. A monument protects a white chunk of granite in Plymouth. On the rock is inscribed "1620."[5] A nearby plaque describes the Pilgrims' landing. But Bradford never mentioned a rock in his writing about the journey, nor did any other person on the *Mayflower*. A large boulder once stood on this spot, but it did not appear in any town records until 1715. Also, a mariner would not likely land a shore boat anywhere near it and risk damaging his craft.

corn field, and several graves. There were large baskets of harvested corn, as well as seed. There was an iron kettle and sawn wooden planks. Either Europeans had already been in the area or goods from their ships had been found or acquired by the Native inhabitants.

Now several miles from the *Mayflower*, the Standish party decided to remain ashore that night. They built a fire and appointed sentinels to watch for intruders. The next day, they cut lengths of cedar wood to bring back to the *Mayflower*. For the first time in a long time, the passengers and crew of the *Mayflower* would enjoy a warm fire. The Standish party also decided to bring the corn to the ship and resolved to return goods to the Nauset in payment when they could.

Plymouth Harbor

In the meantime, the *Mayflower*'s carpenter finished his work on the shallop, which was now seaworthy. Jones took command of the boat for exploration on November 27. He made his way south and then west, following the shore of the cape. For several days afterward, unfavorable weather prevented additional expeditions. On December 6, Jones set out again with Standish and a party of ten settlers, as well as several crew members.[6]

Jones resolved to follow the shore until he found a suitable place for a permanent settlement. He knew from earlier explorers and charts of the area that several suitable harbors were located on the western shore of this wide bay (present-day Cape Cod Bay). He also had to consider the people who already lived there, who might resist the outsiders with force. In fact, this region had once been well populated. But a decade earlier, the Nauset and other peoples living around the bay had suffered a deadly plague brought by contact with Europeans. Much of the Native population had died, and the remaining had abandoned their coastal settlements.

The weather became dangerous. Heavy waves tossed the shallop, and the men froze in the strong, cold winds. A wave splintered the rudder. There was no way to repair the rudder at sea, so the crew put two oars into the water to steer the boat. Then the shallop's mast broke, tumbling into the sea with the sail. The wind and waves forced the shallop toward shore. Night was coming, Jones had no idea where he was, and he could

Pilgrim Places

Cape Cod draws many visitors and is especially busy in the summer. The local towns offer several spots where tourists can retrace the Pilgrims' steps. A good time for a Pilgrim history fan to explore is early November, when the sea and weather are the same as when the *Mayflower* first dropped anchor off Cape Cod.

Pilgrim's First Landing Park in Provincetown marks the spot where the first landing party from the *Mayflower* set foot ashore. Pilgrim Pond, in Truro, is the site where the Standish party made camp their second night on shore. Historical markers indicate the locations of other significant events in the early history of the settlement.

not see clearly the distance to the shore. Finally, the boat landed at a small island.

The next day was clear. The mainland was visible across a mile of open water. The Jones party set out west and landed on the mainland. There, at a place the natives knew as Patuxet, they found two small creeks, flat land suitable for farming, and a steep hill ideal for a stronghold.

The crew of the shallop took soundings in the harbor. It was deep enough for larger ships, including the *Mayflower*. With their provisions running low and the temperatures falling, the party decided to look no further. They would make their way back to the *Mayflower* and bring the rest of the settlers there. They would make their home in a place the English called Plymouth.

Naming Plymouth

Neither Jones nor the Pilgrims named their settlement. Instead, Smith suggested Plymouth as the name for the harbor and nearby shore on his 1616 map of New England. At the time, Plymouth was uninhabited—the native peoples who had lived in the area had suffered a disease epidemic, and they either died or fled. Smith's choice of name as one already in use in England was meant to encourage the English to colonize the site. By coincidence, Plymouth was also the name of the last port the Pilgrims had seen in England.

Historical reenactors aboard the Mayflower II *give a sense of the lives of the crew members on the vessel that transported the Pilgrims to America.*

BACK TO ENGLAND

The *Mayflower* was not the first European ship to sail in Cape Cod Bay or explore the coasts and islands near Plymouth. Smith had arrived from England with a small fleet in 1614. Seeking to establish some trade with the Native Americans there, Smith had left behind one of his officers, Thomas Hunt. But instead of peaceably trading with the Nauset and Patuxet peoples who lived in the area, Hunt took 24 of them captive.[1] He sailed to Spain and sold them as slaves. Hunt's actions greatly angered the Nauset and Patuxet peoples and set them against any further trading or friendship with Europeans.

The Wampanoag

The Pilgrims knew they would not be alone at Plymouth. The Nauset people of the Wampanoag confederacy had villages and farms on Cape Cod. The Wampanoag and other native people had been living in this area for more than 5,000 years.[3] They knew the place where the Pilgrims settled as Patuxet. One of their leaders, Massasoit, first visited the Pilgrim settlement in March 1621. At that meeting, the Wampanoag and the Pilgrims made an agreement not to harm each other, and the Wampanoag agreed not to bring their weapons when the two groups met to trade.

The history that followed was not as peaceful. Many Wampanoag were killed or displaced during King Philip's War (1675–1676), when they fought with the Massachusetts colonists. But the confederation survived. Its descendants now make up two federally recognized Nations, the Mashpee on Cape Cod and the Nation of Gay Head, a community on the island of Martha's Vineyard.

In 1617, native people burned a French ship on Cape Cod and killed or captured its crew. The iron kettle found by Standish and his party may have come from that ship. But since that time, the Patuxet had abandoned Plymouth. Many of them, along with other members of the Wampanoag confederacy, had died of diseases brought by the Europeans.

Becoming Settlers

The Pilgrims who arrived in December 1620 were thankful to survive their journey. Bradford, writing later in his history of the colony, described the settlers as they came ashore for the first time:

> Being thus arrived in a good harbor and brought safe to land, they fell upon their knees and blessed the God of heaven, who had brought them over the vast and furious ocean, and delivered them from all the perils and miseries thereof.[2]

At approximately Christmas 1620, the Pilgrims and the *Mayflower*'s crew began working on the settlement's homes and fortifications. During this time, the *Mayflower* stood at anchor in Plymouth Bay. The winter cold was easier to bear on land, where the settlers and crew members could take shelter from the wind, snow, and freezing rain. But disease ran rampant, both ashore and on the ship. During the winter, the *Mayflower* lost three of its four quartermasters, its cook, and its boatswain. By spring, approximately half of the Pilgrims had died.

Plymouth Colony struggled, but it survived. New ships arrived through the 1620s, bringing new settlers. The colony also managed to keep peaceful relations with the Wampanoag peoples living in the region. The Puritans, meanwhile, established the Massachusetts Bay Colony to the north. In 1691, Plymouth Colony,

The Mayflower Doctor

It was common for ships such as the *Mayflower* to bring aboard a surgeon to look after the crew. Weston hired Giles Heale for the trip to America. Heale earned his license from the Company of Barber Surgeons in 1619. He may have had as many as 100 instruments, as well as books and medicines, in his surgeon's chest aboard the *Mayflower*.[4]

Heale had much to attend to during his time in North America, with most of the Pilgrims and the *Mayflower* crew getting sick that first winter. Heale returned to England with the ship in 1621 and set up an office in London. He died in 1652.

Massachusetts Bay Colony, and other newly settled territories in New England combined to form the province of Massachusetts Bay.

The Journey Home

On April 5, 1621, after helping the Pilgrims through their first winter at Plymouth, Jones gave orders to set the *Mayflower* on its course back to England. One of Jones's crew, the cooper John Alden, decided to stay in Plymouth and take his chances with the settlers. The rest of the crew returned to the ship, eager to begin the voyage home.

The boat would again follow the northern track across the Atlantic Ocean. With a westerly wind blowing, the *Mayflower* made the return journey in less than half the time it took to reach North America from England. On May 9, 1621, the ship returned to its berth in the port of London. Later that year, the *Mayflower* returned to serving as a trading vessel. It was chartered for a voyage to the port of Rochelle, in western France. It returned to England with a load of valuable salt.

Original Route to Virginia

Actual Route to Plymouth

ENGLAND

Southampton
August 5

Plymouth
September 6

London
May 9

Dartmouth
August 12

FRANCE

The *Mayflower* continues on to North America, blown off its original course.

The crew uses the screw jack to repair the *Mayflower*'s cracked beam.

The *Mayflower* encounters a storm.

Provincetown
November 11

Plymouth
April 5

Cape Cod
November 9

THE NEW WORLD

NEW ENGLAND

VIRGINIA

ATLANTIC OCEAN

N
W   E
S

(MASSACHUSETTS)

PROVINCETOWN
November 11

PLYMOUTH
April 5

CAPE COD
November 9

NOEPE
(MARTHA'S VINEYARD)

NATOCKETE
(NANTUCKET)

Southampton, August 5, 1620—The *Mayflower* and the *Speedwell* set sail for North America.

Dartmouth, August 12—The ships stop at Dartmouth for the *Speedwell* to get repairs.

Plymouth, England, September 6—The *Mayflower* and *Speedwell* depart Plymouth, but the *Speedwell* springs a leak and turns back.

Cape Cod, November 9—The crew of the *Mayflower* sights Cape Cod.

Provincetown, November 11—The *Mayflower* anchors at what is now Provincetown, Massachusetts.

Plymouth, North America, April 5, 1621—The *Mayflower* sets out from Plymouth for the return voyage to England.

London, May 9—The *Mayflower* returns to its berth in London.

Jones and His Ship

Jones died in March 1622, less than a year after returning from Plymouth. He was buried near his home in Rotherhithe. His estate, including the portion of his ownership of the *Mayflower*, went to his widow.

By this time, the *Mayflower* was aging. As the ship's hull timbers wore out, they grew troublesome and leaky. The years of strain on rigging, masts, and sails made them more prone to damage. Repairs grew more expensive, and the ship, like all others, gradually lost its value.

For Jones's partners, it was simply a working vessel that was outliving its usefulness. No historical importance was attached to its voyage across the Atlantic Ocean. In fact, the partners may have been unhappy over the loss of their ship for commerce for nearly a year while Jones was making his journey to and from the New World. They never sailed it back to North America after Jones's death.

On May 24, 1624, appraisers in London examined the ship to determine its value. The document that resulted from the appraisal survives in a London archive. According to that appraisal, the *Mayflower* was in ruins and not worth saving.

There was a small inventory of goods and equipment aboard the *Mayflower*. The appraisers found the ship itself, with its hull, masts, yards, shore boats, and windlass, worth 50 pounds (approximately $11,300 today). The five anchors aboard were worth 25 pounds (approximately $5,600 today), and the "more than half-used" sails approximately 15 pounds (approximately $3,400 today). The rigging, including the metal cables and hemp ropes, were valued at 35 pounds (approximately $7,900 today). In addition, there were weapons stowed aboard, including eight muskets, as well as tar pots and a cooking kettle. In all, the ship and its contents were valued at 128 pounds, eight shillings, and four pence, equivalent to approximately 22,000 modern English pounds or $28,543.[5]

After the *Mayflower* was appraised and sold, it was broken up for scrap. Heavy beams, masts, and yardarms could be used as replacement parts on other ships. The anchors and weapons were sold—to whom, nobody knows. No trace of the ship has survived, and no contemporary paintings or drawings of the ship

The Second Mayflower

Alan Villers was an experienced seafaring skipper when he took on a challenging voyage in 1957. The Australian sailor agreed to pilot a replica of the original *Mayflower*, named the *Mayflower II*, from England to Massachusetts. Wearing Pilgrim garb, he set off in April of that year and safely made it across the Atlantic.

The *Mayflower II* made some important changes for the safety and comfort of the crew. The passengers slept in beds, not hammocks. Water was stored in steel tanks, which were more secure against leakage than wooden barrels. Also, the British air force tracked the *Mayflower II*. The ship departed Plymouth, England, on April 20, 1957, and arrived at Plymouth on June 13, 1957. As the vessel neared the coast of Massachusetts, the US Coast Guard helped guide the ship. The voyage was a success, and the *Mayflower II* remains open to the public at its berth in Plymouth, a gift from the British to the United States.

exist. For some time, the *Mayflower* and Jones were forgotten, surviving only in accounts of the voyage by Bradford and others.

The Mayflower *in History*

The *Mayflower*, for a time, was forgotten. No contemporary images of the ship survive, although the Dutch-designed fluyt was a common vessel. As the first English colonies grew in importance in American history, however, legends surrounding the *Mayflower* took root. In England, for example, it was said that parts of the *Mayflower* were used to build structures near London and Harwich. The most famous of these buildings is the Mayflower Barn, located in the village of Jordans, in the county of Buckinghamshire. In 1618, Thomas Russell purchased the surrounding farm. In 1624, the year the *Mayflower* was scrapped, Russell raised or enlarged a barn with timbers bought from a ship. In *The Finding of the* Mayflower, published in 1920, J. Rendel Harris gave evidence that the timber Russell used for his barn came from the *Mayflower*. But the legend of the Mayflower Barn has remained a legend. Most historians investigating Harris's evidence did not find any support for it.

If not for one dangerous voyage across the Atlantic, the *Mayflower* would likely have vanished in history. But its name and image survived as important icons in American history. The *Mayflower* overshadows the forgotten vessels that transported earlier colonists, such as

The Mayflower in Pop Culture ⚓

Thanksgiving

In 1863, Abraham Lincoln proclaimed Thanksgiving as a national holiday in memory of a harvest feast held by the Pilgrims and the Wampanoag in 1621. Celebrated on the fourth Thursday in November, Thanksgiving has become an occasion for families to gather and dine together. Although the Separatists of Plymouth saw their experience in the light of Christian belief and practices, Thanksgiving in modern times is widely seen as a secular holiday.

Words, Music, Movies, and More

Poems, songs, and novels have been written about the *Mayflower*. There have also been several movies, including *Saints and Strangers* and Mayflower: *The Pilgrims Adventure*, starring Anthony Hopkins as Master Christopher Jones. The ship and its passengers have inspired dozens of children's books and *The Mouse on the Mayflower*, a 1968 animated cartoon.

Businesses

A moving company borrowed the ship's name and image, emblazoning the famous fluyt across the side of its big vans. Chatham, a village on Cape Cod, is home to a Mayflower shop, while Washington, DC, has a Mayflower Hotel. And North Carolina boasts a chain of Mayflower Seafood Restaurants. As a name and image, the *Mayflower* is one of history's most famous ships.

The Mayflower's Descendants

Many families can proudly state their ancestors came to America on the *Mayflower*. The descendants of the Pilgrims number in the millions. The General Society of Mayflower Descendants can make the status official. By applying to a historian general, anyone who can prove their lineage from one of the 102 *Mayflower* passengers can join. The society accepts birth certificates, death certificates, marriage papers, genealogies, and legal documents as proof.

Among the more famous *Mayflower* descendants are former presidents George H. W. Bush and George W. Bush, actress Marilyn Monroe, and actor Clint Eastwood.

John Smith, and the Puritans who arrived in New England not long after the Pilgrims. The courage of the Plymouth settlers and the creation of the Mayflower Compact inspired later generations to celebrate them.

Pilgrim monuments are scattered throughout Massachusetts in general and Cape Cod specifically. The Pilgrim Hall Museum welcomes visitors near Plymouth harbor, where a replica of the original *Mayflower* rests at anchor. The entire country celebrates Thanksgiving to mark a harvest feast held by the Plymouth settlers and members of the Wampanoag people in 1621.

The *Mayflower*, built as an ordinary merchant ship, transported so much more than goods. It took a group of outcasts and dreamers far from home and to a place full of promise and possibility, forever changing their lives and the world's history.

Timeline

c. 1600

- The *Mayflower* is built in Harwich, England.

c. 1607

- Christopher Jones and three partners buy the *Mayflower*.

1609

- The Separatists flee England and eventually settle in Leiden, in the Netherlands.
- The first known record of the *Mayflower* is created.

1619

- Facing religious persecution in the Netherlands, the Separatists decide to flee to the Virginia Colony in North America.

1620

- Thomas Weston agrees to finance the voyage of the *Mayflower* and the Separatist settlement in Virginia.
- In September, the *Mayflower* sets out from Plymouth on its journey to North America.
- On November 9, the *Mayflower* reaches Cape Cod in present-day Massachusetts.
- On November 11, Jones and the Separatists sign the Mayflower Compact and agree to search for a permanent settlement site in New England rather than Virginia.
- In December, the settlers establish a colony at Plymouth.

1621

- ⚓ The *Mayflower* sets out on April 5 for England.
- ⚓ The *Mayflower* returns to its berth in London on May 9.
- ⚓ The Pilgrims and members of the Wampanoag people share a harvest feast that is the basis of the Thanksgiving holiday.

1622

- ⚓ Jones dies in March and is buried near his home in Rotherhithe; his portion of ownership of the *Mayflower* is left to his widow.

1624

- ⚓ The *Mayflower* undergoes an appraisal on May 24 to determine its value, which is very little.

c. 1624

- ⚓ The *Mayflower* is broken up, and its useful parts are sold for scrap.

1691

- ⚓ The Plymouth Colony is incorporated into the province of Massachusetts Bay.

Essential Facts

What Happened

The *Mayflower*, a merchant ship under the command of Christopher Jones, transported 102 English colonists to North America in the fall of 1620. These settlers established Plymouth Colony on the western shore of Cape Cod Bay in present-day Massachusetts. This was the second English settlement in North America, founded 13 years after Jamestown, Virginia.

When It Happened

The voyage began on September 6, 1620. The *Mayflower* reached Cape Cod on November 9, and the first landing party went ashore on November 13. The ship returned to England in April 1621 and was broken up sometime after April 1624.

Where It Happened

The *Mayflower* set out from the port of London, England, in the summer of 1620, stopping at the English ports of Southampton, Dartmouth, and Plymouth before setting out to cross the North Atlantic Ocean. The ship followed a northern track to avoid pirates but ran into unfavorable weather that delayed the journey. After arriving at Cape Cod, the *Mayflower* remained anchored off the New England coast until the spring of 1621.

Key Players

⚓ Christopher Jones of Harwich, England, was a part-owner and the master of the *Mayflower*.

⚓ The Pilgrims were two groups of people. One group was the Separatists, part of a religious sect who built a settlement in what is now Massachusetts to observe their faith without interference. The other group were non-Separatists known as Strangers and were workers hired to help build the settlement.

⚓ William Bradford, a Pilgrim and a governor of the Plymouth Colony, wrote an important history of the settlement, titled *Of Plymouth Plantation*, that provides important historical information.

⚓ Thomas Weston was a London investor who lent financial support to the Pilgrims.

Legacy

The *Mayflower* has become a symbol of the quest for religious freedom and democratic government among the English colonists. By carrying the Pilgrims across the Atlantic Ocean to the shores of New England, this ordinary merchant ship played a key role in the early settlement of North America by Europeans. It also lent its name to the Mayflower Compact, signed just before the Pilgrims went ashore at Cape Cod. With this short document, the Plymouth colonists established the principle of rule by consent of the governed.

Quote

"We . . . covenant and combine ourselves together into a civil Body Politick, for our better Ordering and Preservation, and . . . do enact, constitute, and frame, such just and equal Laws . . . as shall be thought most meet and convenient for the general Good of the Colony."

—*The Mayflower Compact*

Glossary

astrolabe

An instrument that measures the angle of certain bright stars, helping the user to determine his or her latitude.

berth

A docking place used by a ship while in port.

boatswain

A ship's officer who is responsible for keeping smaller boats, sails, rigging, and other equipment in order.

capstan

A winch used to raise and lower anchors and other heavy components of the ship.

close-hauled

When sails are brought in as much as possible to the centerline of the boat, placing them at eleven o'clock or one o'clock.

contrary wind

Wind blowing in the opposite direction as a ship's course.

cooper

A crew member whose job is to care for the barrels used to store food and water and to transport cargo such as wine.

demurrage

A charge for time spent in port with cargo aboard.

draft

The distance between the water surface and the bottom of a boat.

following wind

Wind blowing in the same direction as a ship's course.

forecastle
A compartment or structure at the front of a ship, commonly used as crew quarters.

helmsman
A crew member responsible for handling a ship's rudder.

mate
A ship's officer who serves directly under the master or captain.

pilot
A ship's officer responsible for giving steering instructions to the helmsman.

pitch
To roll forward and backward under the force of waves and wind.

quartermaster
A ship's officer responsible for keeping stores of food, water, and other supplies.

shallop
A smaller boat stowed on larger vessels, to be used for shore parties and river navigation.

shoal
A bank or rise of land underwater that poses a danger to ships at low tide or in heavy weather.

sounding
A measurement of water depth at sea.

traverse board
A device for tracking the movements of a ship within a four-hour period.

Additional Resources

Selected Bibliography

Bradford, William. *Of Plymouth Plantation*. New York: Knopf, 2001. Print.

Bunker, Nick. *Making Haste from Babylon: The* Mayflower *Pilgrims and Their World*. New York: Knopf, 2010. Print.

Philbrick, Nathaniel. Mayflower: *A Story of Courage, Community and War.* New York: Viking, 2006. Print.

Further Readings

Lasky, Katherine. *Dear America: A Journey to the New World*. New York: Scholastic, 2010. Print.

Philbrick, Nathaniel. *The* Mayflower *and the Pilgrims' New World*. New York: Puffin, 2008. Print.

Online Resources

To learn more about the *Mayflower*, visit **abdobooklinks.com**. These links are routinely monitored and updated to provide the most current information available.

More Information

For more information on this subject, contact or visit the following organizations:

Leiden Pilgrim Museum

Beschuitsteeg 9, 2312 JT
Leiden, Netherlands
31-71-512-2413
leidenamericanpilgrimmuseum.org

The museum has an exhibit of furniture and other items that were used in this Dutch city at the time of the Leiden Separatists.

Pilgrim Hall Museum

75 Court Street
Plymouth, MA 02360
508-746-1620
pilgrimhall.org

This museum in downtown Plymouth exhibits documents, paintings, weapons, armor, books, and furniture from the time of the Pilgrims.

Plimoth Plantation

137 Warren Avenue
Plymouth, MA 02360
508-746-1622
plimoth.org

A 1600s English village comes to life with homes, shops, a grist mill, and a craft center, as well as a Wampanoag village, at the site of the original Plymouth Colony.

Source Notes

Chapter 1. Arrival in the New World

1. "Voyage of the *Mayflower*." *MayflowerHistory.com*. MayflowerHistory.com, 2017. Web. 4 Sept. 2017.

2. "The Pilgrims." *General Society of Mayflower Descendants*. General Society of Mayflower Descendants, 2017. Web. 4 Sept. 2017.

3. Nathaniel Philbrick. Mayflower*: A Story of Courage, Community and War.* New York: Viking, 2006. Print. 9.

Chapter 2. The Origin of the *Mayflower*

1. Dennis Bryant. "Fluyt." *Maritime Logistics Professional.* Maritime Logistics Professional, 5 Nov. 2013. Web. 4 Sept. 2017.

2. Milja van Tielhof. *The "Mother of All Trades": The Baltic Grain Trade in Amsterdam from the Late 16th to the Early 19th Century.* Boston: Brill, 2002. 185. *Google Books.* Web. 7 Sept. 2017.

3. Leon C. Hills. *History and Genealogy of the* Mayflower *Planters and First Comers to Ye Olde Colonie.* Baltimore, MD: Genealogical Company, 2002. 65. *Google Books.* Web. 4 Sept. 2017.

4. Massachusetts Society of *Mayflower* Descendants. *The* Mayflower *Descendants* XXI (1919): 73. *Google Books.* Web. 4 Sept. 2017.

5. Ibid. 338.

6. Ibid. 73.

7. Ibid. 338.

Chapter 3. The Pilgrims

1. "Captain John Smith Describes the Voyage of the First Colonists in Virginia." *Library of Congress.* Library of Congress, n.d. Web. 4 Sept. 2017.

2. Ibid.

3. Nathaniel Philbrick. Mayflower: *A Story of Courage, Community and War.* New York: Viking, 2006. Print. 19.

4. Ibid.

5. Ibid.

6. Ballard C. Campbell. *Disasters, Accidents, and Crises in American History.* New York: Facts on File, 2008. 9. *Google Books.* Web. 4 Sept. 2017.

7. Leon C. Hills. *History and Genealogy of the* Mayflower *Planters and First Comers to Ye Olde Colonie.* Baltimore: Genealogical Company, 2002. 27. *Google Books.* Web. 4 Sept. 2017.

8. Massachusetts Society of *Mayflower* Descendants. *The* Mayflower *Descendants* XXI (1919): 73. *Google Books.* Web. 4 Sept. 2017.

Chapter 4. Preparing to Sail

1. Nathaniel Philbrick. Mayflower: *A Story of Courage, Community and War*. New York: Viking, 2006. Print. 24.

2. Edward Arber. *The Story of the Pilgrim Fathers, 1606–1623 AD, as Told by Themselves, Their Friends, and Their Enemies*. New York: Houghton Mifflin, 1897. 328. *Internet Archive*. Web. 4 Sept. 2017.

3. Azel Adams. *The* Mayflower *and Her Log, Complete*. Chapter VI. *Project Gutenberg*. Web. 4 Sept. 2017.

4. Beatrice Hudson Flexner. "The Music of the Puritans." *American Heritage*. American Heritage Publishing, 2017. Web. 4 Sept. 2017.

5. Rebecca Beatrice Brooks. "The History of the *Mayflower* Ship." *History of Massachusetts*. Rebecca Beatrice Brooks, 12 Aug. 2011. Web. 4 Sept. 2017.

6. "Inside the *Mayflower*." *MayflowerHistory.com*. MayflowerHistory.com, 2017. Web. 4 Sept. 2017.

7. Nathaniel Philbrick. Mayflower: *A Story of Courage, Community and War*. New York: Viking, 2006. Print. 28.

8. Azel Adams. *The* Mayflower *and Her Log, Complete*. Chapter VI. *Project Gutenberg*. Web. 4 Sept. 2017.

Chapter 5. The *Mayflower* at Sea

1. "What Is the Difference Between a Nautical Mile and a Knot?" *National Ocean Service*. National Oceanic and Atmospheric Administration, 6 July 2017. Web. 4 Sept. 2017.

2. Megan Gambino. "John Smith Coined the Term New England on This 1616 Map." *Smithsonian Magazine*. Smithsonian Institution, 24 Nov. 2014. Web. 4 Sept. 2017.

Source Notes Continued

Chapter 6. Reaching Cape Cod

1. Giles B. Gunn, ed. *Early American Writing*. New York: Penguin Books, 1994. Print. 127.

2. William Bradford. *History of Plymouth Plantation*. Boston, MA: Privately Printed, 1856. 58. *Google Books*. Web. 4 Sept. 2017.

3. "The Journey." *Mayflower Steps*. Mayflower Steps, n.d. Web. 4 Sept. 2017.

Chapter 7. First Explorations

1. "Peregrine White." *MayflowerHistory.com*. MayflowerHistory.com, 2017. Web. 4 Sept. 2017.

2. Nathaniel Philbrick. Mayflower: *A Story of Courage, Community and War*. New York: Viking, 2006. Print. 36.

3. Tom Neale. "Head Over Heels in Love with Islands." *Soundings*. Cruz Bay Publishing, 12 Oct. 2008. Web. 4 Sept. 2017.

4. Nathaniel Philbrick. Mayflower: *A Story of Courage, Community and War*. New York: Viking, 2006. Print. 37–38.

5. Ibid. 38.

6. Ibid. 39.

7. "Famous Cape Cod Shipwrecks." *CapeCod.com*. Cape Cod Broadcasting Media, 18 Apr. 2016. Web. 4 Sept. 2017.

8. Nathaniel Philbrick. Mayflower: *A Story of Courage, Community and War*. New York: Viking, 2006. Print. 41.

Chapter 8. Delaying the Return Journey

1. "Mayflower Compact." *History.* A&E Television Networks, 2017. Web. 4 Sept. 2017.

2. Ibid.

3. "Mayflower Compact: 1620." *Avalon Project.* Lillian Goldman Law Library, Yale University, 2008. Web. 4 Sept. 2017.

4. Nathaniel Philbrick. Mayflower*: A Story of Courage, Community and War.* New York: Viking, 2006. Print. 57.

5. Francis Russell. "The Pilgrims and the Rock." *American Heritage.* American Heritage Publishing, 2017. Web. 4 Sept. 2017.

6. William Bradford. *Of Plymouth Plantation.* New York: Knopf, 2001. Print. 68.

Chapter 9. Back to England

1. "Tisquantum ('Squanto')." *MayflowerHistory.com.* MayflowerHistory.com, 2017. Web. 4 Sept. 2017.

2. Alden T. Vaughan, ed. *The Puritan Tradition in America, 1620–1730.* Hanover, NH: U P of New England, 1972. 47. *Google Books.* Web. 7 Sept. 2017.

3. "Cape Cod: The Nauset Archaeological District—Eastham." *National Park Service.* US Department of the Interior, 31 Jan. 2017. Web. 4 Sept. 2017.

4. Duane A. Cline. "Medical Arts on the *Mayflower.*" *Ancestry.com.* Ancestry.com, 4 Oct. 2000. Web. 4 Sept. 2017.

5. "Probate Inventory of the *Mayflower* (1624)." *MayflowerHistory.com.* MayflowerHistory.com, 2017. Web. 4 Sept. 2017.

Index

About the Author

Tom Streissguth has published more than 100 nonfiction books for young readers, including histories, biographies, and geography books. He lives in Minnesota and travels frequently throughout the United States as well as Europe and Asia.